The Story of Australian Migrant S
From Convicts to '£10 poms'
Guthrie Hutton

One of the most delightful aspects of travel by ocean liner was the use of streamers, strips of coloured paper that formed a fragile link between parting friends. As the ship pulled away they stretched and broke, severing the bond – bon voyage! The ship here leaving Sydney in September 1927 was *Otranto*. She sailed to Australia on her maiden voyage in January 1926 and after serving as a Second World War troopship returned to migrant sailings along with her sister ship *Orontes*.

Further Reading

The following were the principal books used by the author during his research.

Apsley, Lord, *Why and How I Went to Australia as a Settler*, 1925(?).
Artmonsky, Ruth, *P&O, A History*, 2012.
Bremer, Stuart, *Home and Back*, 1984.
Cable, Boyd, *A Hundred Year History of the P&O*, 1937.
Hammerton, James A., and Thomson, Alistair, *Ten Pound Poms*, 2005.
Williams, David L. *P&O Glory Days*, 1998.

Acknowledgements

When we emigrated to Australia in 1954 I went free, too young to be a 'ten-pound pom', but old enough to garner memories that have stayed with me ever since. Family circumstances brought me back to Britain, but I still feel an attachment to the country, pronounce some words with an Australian accent and follow the fortunes of my favourite AFL team, an unlikely enthusiasm given that we first settled in rugby league playing Brisbane, but the school I went to played Aussie Rules and thus introduced me to the greatest footy game on the planet! We moved to Melbourne in 1956 just in time for the Olympic Games, but alas too late for me to get a job selling ice creams in the stadia. I finished my schooling in Melbourne, attended night school and started work. I've been working ever since, if writing little books like this counts as work.

In compiling this collection of pictures and stories, I have been helped by Cath and Ted Rawlings, Val Hinson and Linda Facey, who shared recollections with me. The people I met on the ship and elsewhere all also helped unknowingly to create the memories.

Although this little book concentrates on migration from Britain, people from all over Europe, including many from the communist east, moved to Australia and we rubbed shoulders at school, college and work. They enriched my view of the world and I am grateful to them all.

Barrabool was one of five P&O Branch Line ships that sailed to Australia by way of the Cape in the 1920s and early 30s.

Introduction

The first people to leave the British Isles for Australia mostly did so unwillingly, as convicts. In 1787, under the command of Captain Arthur Philip RN, they travelled in the 'First Fleet' to set up the penal colony. Over the next 50 or so years many more convicts were transported, many in such appalling conditions that some perished, their bodies dumped at sea, forgotten. Initially steeped in depravity, the colony slowly changed and some free settlers chose to make the arduous journey to an uncertain future, adding to a growing population alongside former convicts. The British Government realised that the settlement was there to stay and for it to prosper, more migrants were needed and so established an Emigration Commission in 1831. Different schemes promoted by individual states followed so that through the 19th century more than one million migrants moved to Australia.

The ships that carried emigrants halfway round the world changed dramatically over the years. To begin with they were sail-driven and passengers endured months at sea in often very uncomfortable conditions, traversing some of the planet's wildest seas as they headed round the Cape of Good Hope and across the Southern Ocean. When the Suez Canal opened in 1869 the distance and duration of the journey were significantly reduced, although some ships continued to go around the Cape. There was also an overlap in the transition to steam power with some ships remaining under sail while others used both sail and steam until the latter became the norm.

As the 20th century advanced, ships got bigger and passenger numbers increased. During the First World War many fine vessels were lost and then replaced by even bigger ships. History repeated itself in the Second World War as more liners were sunk. After the war the Australian Government faced the uncomfortable reality that the country could be vulnerable to hostile forces and in response adopted a policy, in partnership with Britain, to promote a very attractive assisted passage migration scheme: a ticket to Australia would cost £10. People quickly took up the offer, but with so many ships lost during the war the ones that were left were barely adequate to cope with the numbers. Again, despite delays caused by a post-war shortage of materials, new and bigger ships were built to meet the growing demand.

For migrants, the journey was the experience of a lifetime, living the high life and visiting countries some had never heard of. On arrival in Australia they faced reality and the prospect of making a new life in a new land that was in some ways familiar, but also very different to the place they had left behind.

Inevitably the assisted passage scheme couldn't last. Air travel became increasingly viable in the 1960s and with the invention of the jumbo jet the days of the big white ships were over, but for a brief golden age some of the finest liners ever built sailed to the southern sun with a complement of passengers that included migrants travelling for a tenner, or less!

A two-berth tourist class cabin on P&O's Arcadia.

The *Success* was 50 years old in 1890 when she became 'The Australian Convict Ship'; a floating museum with exhibits that owed more to lurid fantasy than historical fact. Initially the venture didn't match her name, but by the early 20th century she was sailing the world's oceans showcasing the horrors of transportation. In reality the ship never carried convicts. Built of teak in Burma in 1840 she traded briefly around the Indian sub-continent before new owners used her for a few years to carry British migrants to Australia. One of these trips ended at Melbourne at the height of the gold rush and the crew deserted in search of easy riches. Stranded on the Yarra River, *Success* was one of a number of vessels converted in the mid 1850s into prison ships, so she did have some connection with miscreants before her role as a visitor attraction began. It ended when she caught fire in American waters, burned to the waterline and sank. She had been afloat for 106 years.

The Emigration Commission of 1831 offered assisted passages to selected people and sought certain skills, notably in agriculture. The commissioners chartered ships and expected owners to fit them to a better standard than the awful conditions on many migrant vessels. Young women were needed to redress the population imbalance and married couples were to be placed in accommodation between them and single men. First class passengers were also catered for – they were migrants too. One ship, the *Marco Polo* (*below left*), built in New Brunswick, Canada, looked inelegant, but below the waterline had the shape of a clipper and in 1852 completed the passage in record time. Her skipper, a wily Aberdonian, knew that his first-rate crew of 'wild Irishmen' could desert in Melbourne for the goldfields and so bribed the local police to have them all arrested for mutiny. Thus, when the ship was ready for the return journey, he had a crew that, far from being resentful, seemed to admire his deviousness.

Designed by the famous engineer Isambard Kingdom Brunel, the *Great Britain* (*above*) was an iron-hulled steam and sail-driven ship. Intended for trans-Atlantic service she sailed on her maiden voyage to New York in 1845, but flopped financially and was bought by Gibbs, Bright and Company to carry migrants to Australia, a task she performed between 1852 and 1875. Her robust construction and ability to sail with either the wind or steam, made her ideal for long-haul voyages in variable conditions. She later operated as a cargo carrying sailing vessel until, after lying stranded for years at Port Stanley in the Falkland Islands, she was rescued and towed to Bristol for preservation as a museum exhibit.

Anxious to encourage development, individual Australian states provided assistance to those prepared to make the journey from Britain. In the days of sail this was not the most comfortable experience but George Thomson's Aberdeen Line actively sought to attract passengers. Their clipper ships became well known and their skippers often engaged in races with rivals, with the frequent contests between the *Pericles* (*Left*) and the *Brilliant* generating much interest ashore. Both ships weighed about 1,670 tons and were built in Aberdeen in 1877 to broadly similar dimensions. *Pericles* was a Thomson ship, (they often bore classical Greek names) and was better equipped for passengers, although the return cargo of wool was a good earner too.

The heady days of fast clippers racing under sail were eventually supplanted by steam and although the Aberdeen name remained important to Australia-bound passengers for many years to come, other companies became familiar on the route. One of these was the Orient Line – full name, Orient Steam Navigation Company – established in 1878, although prior to that a forerunner had operated sailing ships, with the first one to be named *Orient* dating from 1850. A new *Orient* was launched in 1879 and at 5,386 tons was the largest steamship built up to that time for the Australian passenger trade. She was fast, setting a new record of 38 days on her maiden voyage to Adelaide by way of the Cape. She is seen here on the left, with the *Austral* of 1881 on the right, both fitted with auxiliary sailing rigs showing that it took a while for owners fully to embrace steam and stop fitting masts and sails to their vessels. The younger *Austral* was scrapped in 1902, but *Orient* remained in service until 1910.

The 6,116 ton *Ormuz* was built at the Fairfield yard in Govan, on the Clyde, and launched in September 1886. Like the two ships on the facing page she was originally fitted with an auxiliary sailing rig, although that had been removed before this picture was taken. In service, she quickly gained a reputation as a fast ship, but also one that had an unfortunate record of hitting other vessels. Homeward bound in the English Channel in January 1900 she ran into the South Shields collier *Glasgow* off Dungeness, sinking her. The crew of *Ormuz* rescued the stricken sailors and landed them in Dover before continuing to Tilbury where damage was assessed as slight. Later that year, while leaving Melbourne, a mistake by the pilot caused her to collide with another ship, the *Ismailia*, at the mouth of Port Philip Bay and this time *Ormuz* had to return to port for repairs. She was sold to a French company in 1912.

For much of the 19th century travelling by ship to Australia was not for the faint-hearted. Ships were small, seas were big and for many people seasickness was a wretched torment until they developed 'sea legs'. In the 1890s the Orient Line sought to ease apprehensions by extolling the virtues of their new ships in a guidebook. It gives some idea of the purgatory endured by those not travelling first class on earlier voyages. They had to bring on board their own bed, bedding and 'mess utensils', a practice consigned to history on the new ships where cabin and table requisites were provided and berths supplied with bedding. Passengers could relax in well-furnished public rooms, although the guidebook reminded would-be travellers that everyone's comfort depended on 'mutual forbearance'. This was especially true of spaces like the music room on the *Osterley*, seen here, where the piano could be a source of discord, even 'torture' if played inconsiderately or just plain badly.

One of the more telling comparisons with the past was in food. Formerly, flavourless, monotonous, dismal fare was served up week after week, the bread was dry, the salt beef was salty and the taste of 'ship's tea' was memorable, but not in a good way. Livestock, carried in pens and coops, could be seen diminishing as the voyage progressed. Steam ships changed all that. They could generate electricity and thus refrigerate food, enabling some passengers to eat better at sea than ashore. Fish, game, milk, butter, fruit and vegetables could be served well away from land. Murray River cod could be eaten while the ship was steaming up the Thames, or the delicate flavour of sole enjoyed while crossing the Indian Ocean. And with electric light, people could see what they were eating. Passengers travelling second class were served meals in dining rooms like the one shown here on the *Otway* with swivel chairs fixed to the deck to ensure they didn't shift in rough weather.

Otway was one of six new ships of just over 12,000 tons ordered by the Orient Line in the early years of the 20th century. She was built at Fairfield's Govan yard but her near sisters were spread around other builders. The London & Glasgow Shipbuilding Company, also of Govan, built *Osterley*, John Brown's yard on the north bank of the river at Clydebank built *Orsova* and the slightly larger *Orama*, seen in this picture. *Otranto* and *Orvieto* were products of Workman, Clark and Company in Belfast. These fine ships all set off on maiden voyages from London to Australia around 1910, but when the First World War broke out in 1914 they were pressed into service of a different kind. *Otway* and *Orama* were sunk while operating as 'armed merchant cruisers' (civilian ships with guns mounted on their decks, naval personnel added to their crew and HMS to the name) and *Otranto*, serving as a troopship, collided with another ship in fog off Islay and sank with the loss of over 480 American soldiers and British seamen. The war ended five weeks later.

Although three of the Orient Line's six new ships were lost during the First World War three survived and one, the *Orvieto*, was written into Australian history, not by conveying people to the country, but taking them away. In the early days of the war she was requisitioned as a troopship by the Australian government and in November 1914 was made flagship for the first convoy carrying the commanding officer and troops of the Australian Imperial Force (AIF) to Egypt. From there they went on to create the ANZAC legend in the hell of Gallipoli. On her way over to Egypt *Orvieto* called at Colombo where she embarked captured men from the German cruiser *Emden*, sunk in the Indian Ocean by HMAS *Sydney*. *Osterley* also worked as an Australian troopship for much of the war and another of the six sisters, *Orsova*, was a British troopship. She was damaged by a mine, beached, repaired and after the war resumed sailings to and from Australia along with *Osterley* and *Orvieto*.

Although the Suez Canal opened in 1869, some companies continued to sail to and from Australia by way of South Africa. One of these was the Blue Anchor Line, but in 1909 their new flagship, *Waratah*, on her second return trip to Britain, left Durban for Cape Town, and disappeared. It remains one of the great, unsolved maritime mysteries, compounded by reported sightings of the *Flying Dutchman*, a ghostly ship and crew forever condemned to sail the stormy seas off the Cape, presaging disaster. It was undoubtedly a disaster for the Blue Anchor Line, but the Peninsular and Oriental Steam Navigation Company (P&O), saw an opportunity. One of the great British shipping companies, in existence since 1837, P&O was keen to operate the route and in 1910 bought the five remaining Blue Anchor ships. The *Beltana* was one of these, seen here sporting the old company's black funnel with a blue anchor painted on a white band, which P&O retained until the First World War.

Under new ownership, the Blue Anchor Line ships continued sailing to and from Australia by way of South Africa on what P&O called their Branch Service, or Branch Line. All except one of the old ships survived the First World War but were replaced in the early 1920s by five new vessels with Australian names beginning with 'B'; *Baradine, Ballarat, Bendigo, Barrabool* and the one seen here at Cape Town, *Baradine*. At just over 13,000 tons these were not small ships, but nor were they luxury liners, they were basic, no-frills, one-class vessels. They could accommodate up to 1,100 migrants, some of who paid the full ordinary fare while others, nominated by friends and approved by the Australian Government, travelled on assisted passages. As competition increased from more comfortable ships on the shorter Suez Canal route, the Branch Line began to lose its appeal and, in the mid 1930s, P&O stopped its South African sailings and scrapped the five 'B' ships.

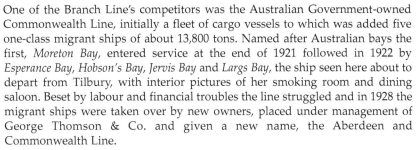

One of the Branch Line's competitors was the Australian Government-owned Commonwealth Line, initially a fleet of cargo vessels to which was added five one-class migrant ships of about 13,800 tons. Named after Australian bays the first, *Moreton Bay*, entered service at the end of 1921 followed in 1922 by *Esperance Bay*, *Hobson's Bay*, *Jervis Bay* and *Largs Bay*, the ship seen here about to depart from Tilbury, with interior pictures of her smoking room and dining saloon. Beset by labour and financial troubles the line struggled and in 1928 the migrant ships were taken over by new owners, placed under management of George Thomson & Co. and given a new name, the Aberdeen and Commonwealth Line.

In 1931, management of the Aberdeen and Commonwealth Line passed to Shaw Savill & Albion, a company with strong links to New Zealand. They moved *Esperance Bay* to their New Zealand service, renamed her *Arawa* and curiously also renamed *Hobsons Bay* as *Esperance Bay*. During the Second World War the 'Bay' ships were requisitioned as troopships, or 'armed merchant cruisers', with perhaps the most famous of these being *Jervis Bay*, seen here in 1931 at Hobart. In November 1940 she was escorting an Atlantic convoy when the pocket battleship *Admiral Scheer* attacked. The old liner was massively outgunned but her captain drove toward the enemy, drawing her fire. Hit several times, she sank, but had given the convoy time to scatter in gathering gloom. Three of the old 'Bays', with their distinctive green-painted hulls, returned to migrant sailings in 1948. *Esperance Bay* (formerly *Hobson's Bay*) was scrapped in 1955 and her remaining sisters went to breakers' yards two years later.

While the Branch Line served Australia by way of South Africa, P&O's main route was always through the Suez Canal. In the years running up to the First World War they introduced ten new two-class ships, all with names starting with the letter M. One of these, pictured here, was the *Mooltan*, a 9,620 ton liner built by Caird & Co. of Greenock and launched in 1905. She continued on Australian sailings during the war years, but often carried people going to the fight including, in 1915, members of the Australian Army Nursing Service. The war claimed six of the 'M' ships including *Mooltan*, torpedoed in 1917 off Sardinia. The need to replace these losses was helped by the company's decision before the war to order two 16,000 ton ships. Construction was delayed by shortages of materials and labour, but *Naldera* and *Narkunda*, entered service in 1920. Another two 16,500 ton liners, *Mongolia*, *Moldavia* and two 21,000 ton ships, *Maloja* and another *Mooltan* joined the fleet in 1923.

Prior to the First World War, the British Government awarded the contract to carry the Royal Mail between Australia and Britain jointly to the P&O and Orient Lines and with the two companies each operating a fortnightly sailing, a fast liner was speeding the mails every week. The war disrupted the service and reduced the company fleets; P&O lost six ships and the Orient Line three. Anxious to reinstate the mail service as soon as possible the remaining vessels were quickly returned to the company fleets and to make up for the losses, three former German ships, which had been transferred to Britain as war reparations were sold to the Orient Line. One of these, the *Zeppelin* of the Norddeutscher Lloyd Line, is seen here in her new colours, renamed *Ormuz*. After a few years sailing on the Australia run she was sold back to her former German owners in 1927 when British shipyards began to deliver new, bigger liners.

The new Orient Line ships of the 1920s were, at 20,000 tons, larger than previous company vessels. They were the *Orford, Oronsay, Orontes, Otranto* and the one seen here, *Orama*. She sailed on her maiden voyage in November 1924 and departed Tilbury again in March 1925. On board were about 150 migrants including a member of parliament, Lord Apsley who wanted to find out what being an assisted passage migrant was really like, so concealed his identity by travelling under another man's name. About 250 Italians also joined the ship at Naples. Food was plain, good and plentiful, and the passengers organised recreations; Lord Apsley's alter ego won the potato race. Through the Migration Bureau in Australia he got manual work breaking new ground on a number of farms and only revealed his true identity when Lady Apsley came out to join him. *Orama* meanwhile shuttled between Britain and Australia, served as a troopship during the Second World War, and was sunk in 1940.

The image of Orient Line ships changed dramatically in December 1934 when *Orion* took to the water at Barrow-in-Furness. And if the ship looked different, the manner of her launch was also new, carried out by the Duke of Gloucester, the Governor General of Australia, using a radio link from Brisbane. The main outward differences were that the company's traditional black hull was replaced with a corn colour, and there were no dummy funnels, which were common at the time, only one real one, and a single mast leaving more deck space for recreation. Inside, instead of hotel-like pastiche impressions of historic styles, interiors were stylish, modern and ship-like. The largest Orient Line ship to date at 23,370 tons, she went back to the Australian run after the Second World War, but was placed on cross-Pacific sailings in 1954. Her sister ship, *Orcades*, sailed on her maiden voyage in 1937, but was sunk in 1942 while serving as a troopship.

A couple of years before *Orion* took to the water, P&O had made an equally significant change to their ships by commissioning two new 22,500 ton, turbo-electric liners from the Vickers Armstrong yard at Barrow-in-Furness. They were named after broad Scottish valleys known as Straths, with the first, *Strathnaver*, seen here on the Suez Canal, launched in February 1931, followed in July of that year by *Strathaird*. They had three funnels, although two were dummies, but the most dramatic aspect of their appearance was that the hulls and superstructure were painted white and the funnels buff, a huge change from P&O's previous colour scheme of black hulls, with a white line, black funnels and buff superstructure. Through the 1930s they carried passengers to and from Australia, acted as troop carriers during the war and had their dummy funnels removed before they returned to peacetime service. Converted to single class ships in 1954, they were broken up in the early 1960s.

Vickers Armstrong built three more 'Straths' for P&O, but although referred to as the 'white sisters' they were not quite the same. *Strathmore* was launched in April 1935 and with only one funnel was outwardly different to the two earlier ships. She was also 1,000 tons heavier and instead of turbo-electric engines was powered by steam turbines. They pushed her along at an average of just over 20 knots beating the previous time taken between London and Bombay. She was effectively a one-off ship with minor differences to the next two liners *Stratheden* and *Strathallan*. They were indeed sisters, launched respectively in June and September 1937. During the war the 'Straths' served as troopships with the youngest of the five, *Strathallan*, torpedoed and sunk off North Africa in December 1942, a sad end for a beautiful new liner that had been in service for only eighteen months before the outbreak of war.

The war came uncomfortably close to Australia and so, conscious of the country's vulnerability, the Federal Government implemented an assisted passage scheme for British migrants. The adult fare was set at only £10, children between the ages of 14 and 18 were charged £5 and those under 14 went free, although the charge for older children was later dropped. It was the bargain of the century and people who took up the offer came to be known as 'ten pound poms'. The British Government agreed to make available old passenger liners released from troop carrying duties. One of these, the *Letitia* (*left*), was built at Govan and launched in October 1924 as a trans-Atlantic emigrant ship for the Anchor Donaldson Line of Glasgow. When the war ended she remained with the Ministry of Transport and because most of their ships were given new names preceded by 'Empire' the old *Letitia*, renamed *Empire Brent*, carried migrants to Australia until 1950. One of them sent this picture postcard (*below*) in 1948.

T.S.S. "EMPIRE BRENT"

Such was the scale of migration from Britain to Australia that a number of old ships were rapidly fitted up to meet demand. One of these was the *New Australia*, a highly appropriate name because migrants were often referred to as 'new Australians'. Built in 1931 as the *Monarch of Bermuda,* she was badly damaged by fire during an initial post-war refit and could have been scrapped, but instead was purchased by Britain's Ministry of Transport. They had her converted to carry 1,600 migrants in one class accommodation and she emerged from the refit with her upper works so completely changed she looked like a new ship. She entered service in 1949 managed on behalf of the ministry by the Shaw Savill and Albion Line, a company with a history of sailings to New Zealand and Australia, and links to the sailing clippers of the old Aberdeen Line as managers of the Aberdeen and Commonwealth line. *New Australia* remained in service carrying assisted passage migrants until 1958.

Three old P&O ships were quickly released for migrant sailings. One of these was the 16,750 ton *Ranchi*, launched in 1925 as one of four sister ships intended for service to Bombay, the Far East and China, but the only one to return after the war, minus one of her two funnels. Refitted as a one class migrant ship for 950 passengers, she sailed on her first trip to Australia in June 1948. Her final voyage in 1953 was not to New South Wales, but to Newport, South Wales and the breaker's yard. The 21,000 ton liners *Mooltan* and *Maloja* of 1923 were also returned and emerged from extensive refits in 1948 as one class vessels for over 1,000 passengers. Amongst those who boarded *Maloja* at Tilbury for her second voyage in October that year were members of the Australian team from the London Olympic Games. Travelling on a one-class ship without the trappings of modern sports people, they joined other passengers in games of deck quoits and gave swimming lessons to youngsters. One migrant, who was just a child at the time, recalls being invited to a party given to honour the team, and having the thrill of briefly wearing the one silver and two bronze medals won by Shirley Strickland, the first Australian woman to win an Olympic medal.

The older P&O ships were not the first to return to service; that was *Stratheden* in 1947. Named after the valley through northern Fife formed by the River Eden, her name and place were briefly united in 1942; while serving as a troopship she carried the Fife-based territorial battalion of the Black Watch (Royal Highlanders) to Egypt by way of South Africa. The men who came from the actual Strath Eden might have had a chuckle over that. The picture is thought to show *Stratheden* being refitted at Barrow-in-Furness. Unlike the older ships she retained accommodation for first and tourist class passengers. Assisted passage migrants travelled tourist class, which was situated at the after end, going down from 'C' deck, which was laid out for games, to 'H' deck where a few cabins were clustered around a cage-like structure that separated them from the access shaft for a cargo hatch. It was the lowest of the low, especially the inside cabins, but there was something exclusive about 'H' deck. The other 'Straths' also sailed again to Australia, *Strathaird* in January 1948, *Strathmore* in 1949 and *Strathnaver* in 1950.

If migrants found the experience of sailing on a big passenger liner daunting, a greater culture shock awaited at the ports of call. Many had never left their local area, let alone the British Isles and yet after a few days at sea they could be sitting at the north end of the Suez Canal gazing at the very un-British waterfront of Port Said. Founded in 1859 and named after Muhammad Said Pasha, Khedive of Egypt who authorised construction of the canal, this was a different kind of town. Compared to damp, temperate Britain, the air was different and there were different sounds, sights and smells. Visa restrictions meant that some passengers had to remain on board, but no matter because the ships sat at pontoons close to the shore so people could watch the ever-changing panorama of daily life, Egyptian style. They could only imagine what wonders were on offer at Simon Arzt, the most conspicuous emporium on the waterfront and one of Egypt's finest, filled with enticing merchandise for tourists.

Passengers who were unable to sample the local atmosphere ashore were not really disadvantaged, because it came to them. Bumboats, small craft laden with wares appeared as if from nowhere to cluster around the ship. People who had done this sort of thing before knew the ropes, literally, because they secured thin lines between the little boats and big ship and, with a basket attached, these acted as a pulley system to carry merchandise and money between seller and buyer. And for those familiar with genteel trading on the British high street, there was another difference: bartering. The traders in their little boats pointed to an article, a customer showed interest, a price was named, disputed, and challenged before a bargain was agreed and a fez or some other souvenir hauled up in the basket. For newcomers it was fascinating to watch and then, emboldened, to participate, and all from the comforting security of a big British ship. Connected by a piece of string, buyers and traders were truly worlds apart.

Another interesting spectacle at Port Said, for those interested in such things, was to watch the ships of all nations that sailed past having navigated the canal. It was not wide enough for ships to sail in both directions at the same time, so they moved through in single file convoys, only passing at designated places. The Suez Canal was a remarkable feat of engineering, carried out under the direction of French engineer Ferdinand de Lesseps. Begun in 1856 it was opened in November 1869, cutting over a thousand miles from the sea routes between Europe, the Far East and Australia. Initially just over 100 miles long, it has since been extended and deepened to serve as a vital global trade artery. But for passengers it could be dull because ships had to move very slowly to avoid damaging the canal banks and the mainly desert scenery didn't match the anticipation of sailing through an ever-changing landscape. Once clear of the canal, ships could return to full speed ahead on the Red Sea.

For passengers unable to go ashore at Port Said the first foreign soil they trod was at Aden on the southern tip of the Arabian Peninsula, later incorporated into Yemen. Annexed by Britain in 1839 it was a key port for Indian Ocean shipping to take on water, refuel and re-victual. The water was stored in reservoirs known as the 'tanks' situated in the Crater area of the settlement (it was the crater of an extinct volcano) and it had a distinctly medicinal taste, just another aspect of shipboard life to get used to. The big passenger ships didn't come alongside a wharf or jetty, but moored at buoys out in the harbour and people went ashore in launches. It was a free port, so they could wander where they wanted and go shopping for all sorts of exotic duty-free goodies. And if Port Said was a new experience for people, Aden was different again, in the appearance of the buildings, the people, their clothes and the way of life – for the curious it was fascinating. And it was hot.

Bombay on the west coast of the Indian sub-continent was hot too, and humid. Unlike the previous ports of call it was a huge seething metropolis with a plethora of new experiences. Not all ships called there, but those that did tied up alongside the Ballard Pier from where passengers could head off on bus or taxi trips to see the sights of the city, including the street markets with their exotic sights, smells, bustle, noise and the chance to watch a cobra, hood extended, rise out of a basket and sway to the music of a snake charmer's pipe. The very large and idiosyncratic 'Old Woman's Shoe' in the Kamala Nehru Park was another of the must-see places on the tourist trail, as was the huge up-market Taj Mahal Hotel, which was the scene of a dreadful terrorist attack in 2008. Bombay has since become better known as Mumbai, a global centre of commerce and technology.

Ships calling at Colombo, at the southern end of the island of Ceylon, moored to buoys out in the harbour. People going ashore got a view of their own ship and others, all very big when viewed at water level from a small launch. Again bus or car trips could be taken to see the sights of Kandy or, more locally, performing elephants and a visit to the Mount Lavinia Hotel, one of those places, like the Taj Mahal Hotel in Bombay, where colonial society met in the days of Empire. Those times were passing when the migrants were on the move. Names have changed; Ceylon became Sri Lanka and was later racked by civil war, and other ports of call have been plagued by wars or insurgency. Such troubles were a few years off and the migrants lounging on the hotel's terrace, looking out across an azure sea and palm-fringed beach must have thought they had arrived in heaven. Cold reality meant they were just passing through and when the time came sallied back to the ship and sailed on to Australia.

BY COMMAND OF
HIS MAJESTY
KING NEPTUNE
LORD OF THE SEAS · SOVEREIGN OF ALL OCEANS · RULER OF THE WAVES

THIS IS TO CERTIFY

that *Guthrie   Hutton*
S.S. "STRATHEDEN"
on board has been duly initiated as a Son of Neptune according to the ancient rites & ceremonies existing from time immemorial.

We hereby grant him Freedom of the Seas and charge all kippers, haddocks and other denizens of the deep from molesting him in any way should he fall overboard.

Given under our Hand on the Equator.

11th October 1954

The longest leg of the journey was between Colombo and Australia, across the Indian Ocean. There was a lot of sea and a lot of sky, impressively large birds and flying fish pretending to be birds. There was also the time-honoured ceremony when the ship crossed the Equator into the Southern Hemisphere. Known as 'Crossing the Line' this was usually an occasion for all sorts of high jinks and for certificates to be handed out to commemorate the occasion, and while all that was going on the ships just ploughed on, ever southwards. It was a time for frequent visits to the little salt-water swimming pool and games. Deck quoits played with a rope ring was popular, as was deck tennis. The lines of the court were painted on the deck and the quoit was thrown back and forth over a head high net, and a player had to return it quickly or be penalised for holding on too long.

An ocean liner was a curious thing. Such ships no longer exist, aircraft have taken over their role of shifting people around the world and modern cruise liners don't operate regular schedules on specific routes. With more than 1,000 passengers and crews of over 500 they were like small towns on the move. On dry land folk went about their daily lives oblivious of these transient communities, but all day and all night the liners ploughed on, while people on board ate, slept, relaxed in deck chairs or engaged in a variety of activities like the potato race seen here. People read, wrote letters, sketched and played board games or cards. More organised social events were laid on. Dances were popular as was horse racing. These did not of course feature real horses, but wooden cut outs about the size of a large dog with a rope stretched across the recreation hall to a windlass. Bets were placed and participating passengers wound in the rope as fast as they could, generating much excitement and laughter.

After the long Indian Ocean passage the ships pulled in at Fremantle, the first sight migrants had of Australia. The harbour was situated at the mouth of the Swan River with Victoria Quay as the main berth for passenger ships like Norwegian *Skaubryn* seen here arriving in 1954. She was originally laid down in 1950 as a cargo vessel, but her owner changed his mind and completed her as a passenger ship for European migrants. She was heading for Fremantle again on 31st March 1958 when she caught fire and, after a successful rescue effort, sank, giving her the unhappy distinction of being the only vessel lost at sea during the history of post-war migration to Australia. That was a future trouble, and on this happier occasion the number of people lining the railings to see their new homeland have given her a distinct list to starboard. Passengers not ending their voyage at Fremantle could take the time in port to go on a tour to Perth, the capital of Western Australia some twelve miles away. Then it was back aboard heading east.

Some ships called at Adelaide, the capital of South Australia, but migrant vessels often drove straight across the Great Australian Bight to Melbourne, capital city of Victoria. It is a significant port with extensive docks on the River Yarra, but the large passenger ships tied up at Station Pier at Port Melbourne, the substantial structure in this picture jutting out into Hobson's Bay. It could accommodate a number of large ships at any one time – that could be an Orient liner on the right – and crew members sometimes met friends from other ships lying alongside at the same time. The pier was close to the city centre, so people who were going on up the east coast could visit some of the sights, like the spectacular war memorial on St Kilda Road and Captain Cook's cottage, brought from Yorkshire and re-erected in Fitzroy Gardens. It was a reminder, for British migrants at least, of their country's part in Australia's colonial history, which in some small measure they were adding to.

Arriving by ship in Sydney Harbour was awesome, with wonderful views and the thrill of sailing under that most spectacular of bridges and wondering if the masts would hit. They cleared it of course and having done so large P&O ships, like Strathaird in this picture, came alongside at Pyrmont. This was the final destination for many migrants, although some stayed on board if the ship was continuing on to Brisbane. As passengers got off, wharfies, dressed in the 'uniform' of faded blue, sweat-stained singlet and khaki shorts came on board to unload cargo, which these large passenger ships also carried. Amongst the crates and boxes, were tea chests from India and when one was accidentally holed by a wharfie's hook some of the contents were liberated for a cuppa (yes, dear reader it did happen!). Ships stayed in Sydney for a while, so Brisbane-bound passengers were able to go into the city or take trips to the Blue Mountains and other local attractions.

Some ships went north from Sydney up the east coast and along the Brisbane River to Hamilton Wharf, seen here from *Stratheden* arriving in 1954. This was journey's end and the start of a new life for Queensland-bound migrants. In the state capital, Brisbane, they found a thriving metropolis with city streets that would not have looked out of place in Europe and an impressive tall-towered town hall. The river, and by extension the city, was named by a Lieutenant John Oxley in 1824, after the then Governor of New South Wales, Sir Thomas Brisbane. Oxley perhaps ignored or overlooked the probability that the local Aborigines could already have a name for it. He had been tasked with finding a suitable site for a convict settlement. An initial colony was begun at Redcliffe on Moreton Bay, but quickly abandoned in favour of the spot on the river where Oxley had landed. In fifteen years of existence it gained a reputation for brutality, but from that unpromising start the modern city grew.

British migrants often expected Australia to be similar to home, an English-speaking country, but with more sunshine. In many ways it was, but it was also a vast place with marked differences across the continent and between city and country, and for those arriving in Brisbane it wasn't quite like Britain as this 1970s view of Sandgate Road shows. 'Queenslanders', weatherboard houses with verandas were set on stilts and roofed with corrugated iron. Silver-painted trams ran on streets, some of which were lined with purple-flowering jacaranda trees. Palm trees and eucalypts grew elsewhere. It was mainly hot, sunny and dry, but it could rain hard and heavy, drumming loudly on those tin roofs. Insects were omnipresent and not just the flies that have become a caricature of Australia, there were mosquitos, flying cockroaches, big hairy spiders, many varieties of ants, numerous other beasties and the discordant sound of cicadas. Animals too were unfamiliar and included a variety of lizards, snakes and their laughing nemesis, kookaburras.

Some other things felt strange; Christmas was in mid-summer, daylight changed quickly to night and seasonal changes were slight, but the more tangible experience of going to the well-stocked shops was an eye-opener. Some exotic foods like pineapples, papaws, passion fruit and sweet potatoes have since become familiar in Britain, but to post-war migrants were new and plentiful. Watermelons were very big and in gardens, people grew flowers and other fruits including lemons, bananas, mangos, custard apples and Queensland nuts (macadamias). In the absence of a refrigerator, food could be kept cool with blocks of ice in an icebox. Children ran around in bare feet, and it wasn't a sign of poverty. They carried schoolbooks, not in a satchel but a small case known as a 'port'. Small utility trucks were 'utes'. Urban areas spread out for miles and beyond these the country was big, wide, dry and dusty, roads were long, not metalled and distances were vast, and for some migrants it took a lot of getting used to. For others it was exciting.

Migrants on the assisted passage scheme came from all backgrounds in post-war austerity Britain. Some left bomb-damaged cities, others the smoke and grime of industrial towns, poor rural housing or country villages. All sought new opportunities in a new land, but before that, they spent time together in the close confines of a ship. The first sight of these great vessels was awe-inspiring, usually up close at the dockside. Once inside everything was strange, decks were slightly off level, staircases steep and strangely angled, and there was a distinctive smell and constant low-level sound. Cabins had bunk beds with raised sides and were looked after by stewards who greeted occupants with morning tea. In the dining room, tables had raised edges to prevent things sliding off in heavy weather and once seasickness had been conquered many migrants probably ate more and better food than they had done ashore. These ships were like palaces. The one seen here, launched by Vickers Armstrong at Barrow in October 1947, is the Orient Line's first post-war liner the 28,000 ton *Orcades*, her name reviving that of the ship lost just five years earlier.

During the war Orient Line losses were heavy and when peace returned, the fleet consisted of only the old *Orontes* and *Otranto*, the even older *Ormonde*, and the *Orion* of 1935. By war's end the P&O and Orient Lines were closely aligned. Toward the end of the First World War, P&O's shareholding in the Orient Line had increased to 51 per cent and by the end of the Second World War the two companies were effectively operating as one. It took a while for shipping services to return to what they had been. Both companies built big new ships with broadly similar specifications so that they could co-ordinate fortnightly sailings with interchangeable vessels and as they came into service, and took over from the old reconditioned ships that had fulfilled the immediate post-war need, the pace of migration steadied. The Orient Line's second new ship, *Oronsay*, also built at Barrow-in-Furness by Vickers Armstrong, is seen here in April 1951, just prior to her maiden voyage.

As with the Orient Line, new P&O ships were built to replace wartime losses. The first one to join the P&O fleet, the 28,047 ton *Himalaya* was built by Vickers Armstrong at Barrow-in-Furness and sailed on her maiden voyage in October 1949. Her geared steam turbine engines and twin screws pushed her along at 22 knots, a speed fast enough for a former crew-member to recall her overtaking one of the 'Strath' ships over the course of a day, and the 'Straths' were regarded as fast when they were built. *Himalaya* reduced passage times on all stages of the route, cutting days off the journey between Britain and Australia. Her greater speed and that of subsequent new ships helped when the Suez Canal was closed in 1956 and ships had to be rerouted for a time round the Cape, an addition of 1,200 miles, which would have added many days at sea for one of the older vessels.

Although the assisted passage scheme was originally intended for British migrants, other European nationalities were also soon making the journey in ships like those of Flotta Lauro Line from Italy. With their white hulls and superstructure, blue funnels with a black top and adorned with the company's white star they became a familiar sight in Australian ports. The *Surriento* seen here in the upper picture was originally the USS *Barnett*, an American Marines attack transport ship, before being acquired in 1948 and converted into a passenger ship of 10,700 tons. Her migrant-carrying role spanned the years 1949 to 1955. She was joined in that service by the *Roma*, a slightly larger ship of 14,690 tons, which had been a Royal Navy support aircraft carrier, HMS *Atheling*, built in America and made available to Britain the under the wartime lend-lease scheme. Following extensive conversion to a civilian passenger ship she began migrant sailings from Genoa and other European ports in 1951.

The launch of a commercial passenger liner by a reigning monarch was unusual, so there was great excitement at Harland & Wolff's Belfast yard when Her Majesty, Queen Elizabeth II launched Shaw Savill and Albion's new 20,200 ton liner *Southern Cross* on 17 August 1954. She sailed on her maiden voyage on 29th March 1955. Breaking with hitherto common practice she had no cargo space other than for stores, but more dramatically, as this picture shows, her machinery and funnel were placed aft, like those on a tanker: eyebrows were raised. The company did not deploy her on a shuttle to and from Australia, but maintained their links with New Zealand by sailing around the world and including the country in her itinerary. She had eight decks with public spaces on the upper two, open promenade decks along both sides and two swimming pools with one indoors that was popular in colder climates.

There was accommodation for 1,160 passengers on *Southern Cross*, all in tourist class. The cabins were on the six lower decks and ranged from single berth to six-berth, like the one shown in this picture. There was air conditioning to cabins and all public passenger spaces, which included lounges, smoke room, cinema, tavern, writing room and library. Children were catered for with a recreation room and an infant play area, and diners could eat in one of two restaurants positioned either side of a central galley. Such was the success of *Southern Cross* that the company ordered another ship, this time from Vickers Armstrong at Barrow-in-Furness. Named *Northern Star*, she was 4,500 tons bigger than *Southern Cross* but looked similar with the machinery and funnel aft. Her maiden voyage in July 1962 was seriously disrupted by engine failure, but for much of the 1960s she and *Southern Cross* operated round the world voyages travelling in opposite directions.

A unique double launch was performed on 14th May 1953 by the sister-in-law wives of Donald Anderson, deputy chairman of P&O and his brother Sir Colin Anderson director of the Orient Line. On that day they sent two 30,000 ton liners, P&O's *Arcadia* and the Orient Line's *Orsova*, down the slips at Clydebank and Barrow respectively. For some time the two companies had built their ships at Barrow so it was something of a departure for P&O to order a new liner from John Brown's Clydebank yard. They were not disappointed and indeed senior figures at P&O and John Brown's shared a modest bet with the chairman of the Orient Line that the first of the two to enter service would be the *Arcadia*. She was, sailing on her maiden voyage from Tilbury to Australia on 22nd February 1954. A worthy successor to the great Clydebank-built Cunarders, she was a splendid ship fitted out to a standard that migrants on earlier ships could only dream of.

The almost inevitable merger of the P&O and Orient Lines took place in 1960 after which the hulls of Orient Line ships were painted white. Before that happened, the principal distinguishing feature of *Orsova*, the Orient Line ship launched on the same day as P&O's *Arcadia*, was that she had no navigation masts, only cargo handling stanchions. She sailed from Tilbury on her maiden voyage in March 1954 and on a later voyage that year carried the England cricket team, known at the time as the MCC, to Australia for the 1954/55 Ashes series. Although they travelled first class, the captain, Len Hutton, and other members of the touring party went to talk to passengers in the tourist class section, so cricket enthusiasts amongst the migrants got to meet them and hear how they were going to beat the Aussies, which they did, three matches to one. When the team left Tilbury a woman gave the captain a sprig of heather, evidently a lucky one.

The England cricket team for the Ashes tour in 1958/59 travelled on the *Iberia* but this time were well beaten by Australia, losing the series 4-0 with one match drawn. Perhaps they should have gone on another ship, *Iberia* had a reputation for things going wrong. Effectively a sister ship to *Arcadia*, but with slight differences, she was launched by Lady M'Grigor, wife of the First Sea Lord, Admiral Sir Roderick M'Grigor in January 1954 and sailed from Tilbury on her maiden voyage on 28th September, arriving at Sydney on 1st November. She had 674 first class and 733 tourist class berths. The public spaces in both classes were similar to those on *Arcadia* and included a veranda café, smoking room, dance floor, cinema, dining room and the tourist class lounge seen in this picture. As well as sailings to and from Australia, *Iberia* was used on Mediterranean cruises and in the summer of 1958 became the first British cruise liner after the Second World War to enter New York harbour to the traditional welcome of aeroplanes, boat sirens and fire barges shooting jets of water into the air.